EPIC SURGE

Eastern Iowa's Unstoppable Flood of 2008

(c) 2008, Gazette Communications Inc.
ISBN 978-1-60702-297-8

Gazette Communications
500 Third Ave. SE
Cedar Rapids, Iowa 52401
(319) 398-8211

The Gazette
gazetteonline.com

Table of Contents

LEFT: House on Second Avenue SW, Cedar Rapids, the afternoon of Friday, June 13. (Cliff Jette/The Gazette)

Gary Nelson edged out the second-story window of his Cedar Rapids apartment, while Mason Ayers-Berry (top) assisted and Guy Ayers-Berry (bottom) piloted the boat on Thursday evening, June 12. *(Jonathan D. Woods/The Gazette)*

*N*obody ever thought...

"That was the echo of Cedar Rapids. Nobody ever thought." So said Ron Witt in August 2008. That was while he was helping clean the then-closed Double Inn Bar and Grill in northwest Cedar Rapids. He had worked there as kitchen manager two months earlier. Before the flood.

Nobody ever thought something like this could happen here, something that could leave so many homes and businesses in ruins, so many lives in turmoil. Something that could leave communities facing hard choices about their immediate and long-term futures.

Yes, a river runs through Cedar Rapids. Yes, a river runs through Iowa City and Coralville, rivers run through Eastern Iowa. They've flooded before and they'll flood again. But this thing in 2008, this was far different. This was unreal.

"Never in a million years did we think that we'd be dealing with this magnitude of an event," Iowa City Manager Michael Lombardo said two days before the Iowa River crested at a record level in his city on June 15, basically cutting his community in half.

"I just can't believe it. You caught me at a time when I just don't have the words," Cedar Rapids City Council member Brian Fagan said June 12, a day before the Cedar River crested in his city at a whopping 19 feet above flood level and more than 11 feet beyond the previous record. But when Fagan stated his shock, incredible and vast damage already had been done there.

Nobody really had the words. Nobody ever thought.

All right, let's frame this with a positive, something to be forever treasured. This wasn't another Hurricane Katrina when it came to loss of life. Flood-related deaths were amazingly few in Iowa. Our flooded neighborhoods became ghost towns, but thankfully, without ghosts.

When it came to the harm left behind, however, New Orleans and Cedar Rapids ran neck and neck. The television images and wire-service photographs of Cedar Rapids' flooding were beamed around the world. They led many to describe the disaster as a mini-Katrina. It was far more than "mini" here, though.

Because of a winter filled with brutal snowstorms followed by a wet spring, Eastern Iowa's ground was saturated and its creeks were full. Then rains were heavy and widespread in the first 10 days of June. The Cedar flooded in Cedar Falls and Waterloo, reaching a record 6 feet above its previous high.

The potential of what was headed southward put pits in our stomachs. The American Red Cross opened shelters in Cedar Rapids and Iowa City on June 10. Residents of low-lying neighborhoods in Cedar Rapids were told to be prepared to evacuate.

June 11 was helter-skelter in Cedar Rapids. Sandbagging was a four-quadrant activity. Residents in the city's 100-year flood plain, and then 500-year flood plain, faced mandatory evacuations. The city's bridges were closed and Interstate 380 became the only way across the Cedar.

By the morning of June 12, those pits in the stomachs had twisted into large knots. Like Vinton and Palo to the north, Cedar Rapids had been devastated by the Cedar. Downtown was flooded. All the city's bridges over the river were closed, with Interstate 380 the city's only way across.

It was a full-fledged, mind-blowing catastrophe. The Cedar Rapids Fire Department launched rescue boats on First Avenue West, about 10 blocks from the Cedar. Residents were rescued from roofs of their homes. Members of the Iowa National Guard and U.S. Coast Guard were deployed here. It was surreal.

Many among the thousands of displaced residents were whisked from their residences with little more than the clothes they were wearing.

With electricity cut off in the flooded areas, the city's skyline was dark that night and would be for weeks. Because of traffic congestion, it was a creepy crawl over downtown on I-380 during the day, and just plain eerie at night with the only illumination provided by vehicles' headlights.

The floods of 2008 belonged to Eastern Iowa and the entire state, but Cedar Rapids was its face to the world. The pictures of the water and the nine square miles of deluged area in the city left indelible images.

"If it were an earthquake, it would be a 9.2," said Cedar Rapids City Manager Jim Prosser.

This truly was an epic surge.

DISBELIEF

$\mathcal{W}$e hadn't seen this before here. No one had.

It couldn't be fully comprehended. Maybe it never will.

Eastern Iowa, with rivers of considerable size like the Cedar, Iowa and Wapsipinicon, had seen its share of floods. Those in 1993 were especially nasty. But what plagued the region in the second week of June 2008 stretched belief.

It's not like Cedar Rapids wasn't geared for its all-time worst flood. On Monday of that week, the Cedar was projected to crest there at 22.5 feet. The crest was 19.27 feet for the river's flood of 1993 in Cedar Rapids. The city's record had been 20 feet, set in 1929 and 1951.

The next day, the projection was raised to 24.5 feet, twice the flood level. For the river to reach the city's 500-year flood plain, it had to reach 26.5 feet.

Who had flood insurance for property 10 blocks from the river, or five or even two? Who would have seen a need?

That was answered when Wednesday's revised forecast was 28 feet. When Friday's crest came at 31.2 feet, Cedar Rapids already had faced an unreal reality for more than a full day. Downtown, east of the river, was flooded. Water was deeper and more widespread to the west of the Cedar.

Those directly affected by flooding never will need to be told of its power. Those who watched television reports from a safe distance were jolted repeatedly by the sights.

When two bridges built more than a century ago could be taken out by a flood, you know life in a region is severely changed.

The 793-foot CRANDIC railroad bridge in Cedar Rapids crumbled from the seemingly supernatural force of the Cedar on Thursday of that punishing week.

About 20 miles downstream the next day in the unincorporated Johnson County village of Sutliff, a large portion of the 110-year-old Sutliff Bridge was ripped away. The 827-foot pedestrian bridge, closed to autos since 1981, is on the National Register of Historic Places.

"Emotionally, it's a hole. It's left a hole right in everybody's heart," said Randy Brannaman, president of the Sutliff Bridge Association.

Emotional holes were left about everywhere near Eastern Iowa's angry rivers. One particular word was used repeatedly by those who saw the damage.

Unbelievable.

The Gazette's front page,
Saturday, June 14, 2008

LEFT: Cedar Rapids as the Cedar River neared its crest shortly before noon on Friday, June 13. *(The Gazette/Liz Martin)*

OPPOSITE PAGE: A car abandoned on Third Avenue SE in downtown Cedar Rapids between First and Second streets the morning of Thursday, June 12, was overtaken by the rising Cedar River. *(Liz Martin/The Gazette)*

ABOVE: En route to investigate a report of two people trapped in a mobile home, Cedar Rapids firefighter Dan Dall eased his boat away from dry ground on Ely Road SW near Old River Road SW in Cedar Rapids early Friday morning, June 13. *(Jonathan D. Woods/The Gazette)*

RIGHT: The Cedar River reached its peak along residential Second Avenue SW in Cedar Rapids the afternoon of Friday, June 13. *(Cliff Jette/The Gazette)*

OPPOSITE PAGE: Cruise Apartments Property Manager Tim Furman threw his hands in the air as more rain began to fall along Dubuque Street in Iowa City on Sunday, June 8. Furman and other people from the company were sandbagging to try to preserve an access road for their tenants at the Cliff Apartments. At the time, it appeared as though the worst flooding in Linn and Johnson counties would be in Iowa City and Coralville. *(Brian Ray/The Gazette)*

ABOVE: Bill Garner and Dave Anderson paddled back to the AT&T building on Highway 6, otherwise known as the Coralville Strip, as floodwater from Clear Creek and the Iowa River rose in Coralville on Friday afternoon, June 13. The crest still was to come. *(Jonathan D. Woods/The Gazette)*

LEFT: Iowa River floodwater surrounded the Heartland Inn on Highway 6 in Coralville, where the "Liberty Herky" statue appeared to be on higher ground than an abandoned car on Monday, June 16. *(Jonathan D. Woods/The Gazette)*

OPPOSITE PAGE: Neighbors Tom Melsh (left, behind the chain-link fence) and Rick Hobson were in awe on Friday, June 13, of the water rushing down J Street in southwest Cedar Rapids that flooded both their homes. *(Courtney Sargent/The Gazette)*

LEFT: Nurses Lisa Mahoney (left) and Lori Russell took a needed break during sandbagging at Mercy Medical Center in Cedar Rapids the afternoon of Thursday, June 12. *(Jonathan D. Woods/The Gazette)*

BELOW: Cedar Rapids firefighters Jason Lopez (left) and Jeremy Wagner on Second Avenue SW heading toward the Interstate 380 overpass in Cedar Rapids on the afternoon of Friday, June 13. *(Cliff Jette/The Gazette)*

OPPOSITE PAGE: Powerless, the downtown Cedar Rapids skyline cast an eerie reflection on the floodwater that surrounded it at midnight Friday, June 13. *(Courtney Sargent/The Gazette)*

ABOVE: Larry McMahon (left) and Kent Kilpatrick bailed water from Mercy Medical Center's front entrance in Cedar Rapids on Thursday afternoon, June 12. Nurses and other hospital employees sandbagged while maintenance personnel got a pump started. *(Jonathan D. Woods/The Gazette)*

LEFT: The Veterans Memorial Building (Cedar Rapids City Hall), photographed early Friday, June 13. *(Jim Slosiarek/The Gazette)*

OPPOSITE PAGE: Like many others driven from their homes by flooding, Ronald Austin took refuge at a Red Cross shelter at Viola Gibson Elementary School in Cedar Rapids. Austin, photographed on Sunday, June 15, was displaced from his Geneva Tower home. *(Courtney Sargent/The Gazette)*

ABOVE LEFT: The flood showed no mercy on Cedar Rapids landmarks, overturning the Paramount Theatre's Wurlitzer theater organ. Floodwater also lifted part of the orchestra pit onto the stage, which buckled. Photographed on Tuesday, June 17. *(Liz Martin/The Gazette)*

BELOW LEFT: Floodwater in the Time Check neighborhood, in northwest Cedar Rapids, carried a shed from Jonathan and Lindsay Lawrence's yard to a spot between their home and a neighbor's home. Photographed on Friday, June 20. *(Liz Martin/The Gazette)*

OPPOSITE PAGE: A Iowa National Guard Humvee was stationed at water's edge on Second Avenue SW in Cedar Rapids the afternoon of Friday, June 13. *(Cliff Jette/The Gazette)*

RIGHT: Boathouses from the Ellis boat harbor and other debris smashed against a railroad bridge near Cedar Rapids' Time Check neighborhood in northwest Cedar Rapids on Monday, June 16. *(Brian Ray/The Gazette)*

BELOW: A garage roof rested against a home on C Street SW that same Monday after floodwater began receding in Cedar Rapids. Floodwater almost reached the top of the second-story windows of this home at the intersection with 18th Avenue SW. *(Liz Martin/The Gazette)*

OPPOSITE PAGE: Debris ransacked by floodwater was piled higher than most vehicles along Thompson Drive in Palo when flood recovery efforts were under way Friday, June 27. *(Jonathan D. Woods/The Gazette)*

ABOVE: A roll of toilet paper soaked in mud in the basement bathroom of Olivet Presbyterian Church, 237 10th St. NW, Cedar Rapids. Photographed Tuesday, June 17. *(Courtney Sargent/The Gazette)*

RIGHT: Volunteers like Bret Loes, a teacher from Washington, D.C., came to Iowa to help clean the mess. Loes helped gut the basement of St. Wenceslaus Church, 1224 Fifth St .SE, Cedar Rapids, on Thursday, June 19. He felt compelled to help after seeing the effects of the flood. So he drove to Iowa and started volunteering. *(Jonathan D. Woods/The Gazette)*

DEVASTATION

The numbers are astounding, yet they can't tell this story.

How could you really put a price tag on a long-time home lost to a flood? How could you create and build a business with a sound plan and hard work, then simply assign a monetary figure to your loss when an unnatural natural disaster wiped you out?

Raw statistics can never capture raw pain. But the numbers from the floods of Eastern Iowa are too spectacular to be dismissed.

The late-summer 2008 estimates showed Cedar Rapids with flood-damaged homes worth $231 million. Forget the money for a moment and consider this: In a city of about 120,000 residents, 5,390 homes were harmed by this disaster, many irreparably.

That $231 million total resonated in Iowa City, too. It was close to the estimated $232 million in flood damage at the University of Iowa.

"I knew it would be a big number," UI President Sally Mason said. "I still gulped when I heard it."

Gulp-worthy data could fill this book. Cedar Rapids had 1,049 damaged businesses, totaling $560 million. An additional 310 public buildings and facilities were affected, with damages of $569 million.

The toll in Palo, a Linn County town of 950, was $25 million. All but 10 of the 423 homes in the community along the Cedar had flood damage. Many families moved into recreational vehicles and tents.

"We're talking about long-term trauma," said Penny Galvin, who coordinated volunteer efforts in Palo.

Trauma flowed through the area after floodwaters receded. In Cedar Rapids, city and county government took many different temporary homes, wondering how temporary they actually might be.

City Hall, the Linn County Courthouse, the main Cedar Rapids Public Library, the Cedar Rapids Police Station, the Linn County Jail — all are near the Cedar River or on May's Island in the river. All were rendered unusable by the flood, like most structures in town that lined the Cedar.

No, dollar figures can't describe what the flooding has done to this region's psyche. But here's another, anyhow:

The estimated flood damage to Linn County alone is $1.657 billion.

Gulp.

The Gazette front page,
Tuesday, June 17, 2008

OPPOSITE PAGE: Adam Pledge of Cedar Rapids dug in, carrying waterlogged sofa cushions from his parents' Time Check home in northwest Cedar Rapids the morning of Friday, June 20. Pledge, an employee in the city's solid waste department, also picked up trash removed from flood-damaged homes in the recovery effort. (Liz Martin/The Gazette)

OPPOSITE PAGE: Evan Vulich (right) helped clean up the H.D. Youth Center & Restaurant, 1006 Third St. SE, Cedar Rapids, on Saturday, June 21. *(Jonathan D. Woods/The Gazette)*

ABOVE: Stools removed from the waterlogged Piano Lounge in downtown Cedar Rapids were put on the sidewalk to dry on Tuesday, June 17. *(Liz Martin/The Gazette)*

RIGHT: Tommy Bruner sorted through flood-damaged possessions at the home he rents on E Avenue NE in Cedar Rapids on Wednesday, June 18. His basement was flooded and a couple of inches of water covered the first floor. *(Cliff Jette/The Gazette)*

ABOVE: An aerial view of where the Cedar River passes by the Penford Products Co. plant shows the Cedar River is rising but business as usual and the CRANDIC railroad bridge intact on Wednesday, June 11. The Eighth Avenue bridge is to the right. *(Cliff Jette/The Gazette)*

RIGHT: Two days later, on Friday, June 13, the Cedar was wreaking havoc. *(Liz Martin/The Gazette)*

OPPOSITE PAGE FAR RIGHT: Pressure from the flooding was intense. A ruptured grain silo knocked over rail cars at the Cargill plant near Cedar Lake in Cedar Rapids on Sunday, June 15. *(Jim Slosiarek/The Gazette)*

OPPOSITE PAGE: A boat ended up on the front porch of a Fourth Street NW home in the Time Check neighborhood. Photographed Friday, June 20. *(Liz Martin/The Gazette)*

LEFT: Televisions await pickup in front of a home on A Avenue NW on Thursday, June 26. *(Liz Martin/The Gazette)*

ABOVE: Ron Douglas cleans out his home on A Avenue NW in Cedar Rapids on Wednesday, June 18. Water reached the top of the door on the first floor. *(Cliff Jette/The Gazette)*

OPPOSITE PAGE: Capt. Dan Cougill, an Iowa Task Force 1 member and Sioux City firefighter, was part of a strike team in southwest Cedar Rapids when he checked a Czech Village home for flood damage on Monday, June 16. Nine teams had spread out across the flood-damaged areas to check for structural integrity before residents and employees could return. *(Liz Martin/The Gazette)*

ABOVE: A wooden deck ended its flood journey on the front steps of a Czech Village home as floodwater receded. Photographed Monday, June 16. *(Liz Martin/The Gazette)*

RIGHT: A mud-caked toy horse and other belongings in a Time Check home in northwest Cedar Rapids. Photographed Friday, June 20. *(Liz Martin/The Gazette)*

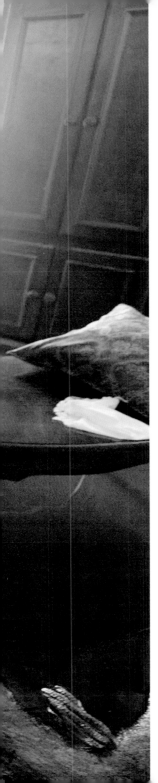

OPPOSITE PAGE: Delores Korsmo of Cedar Rapids' Rompot neighborhood surveyed her damaged living room on Saturday, June 14, after the house took about 3 1/2 feet of water in the flood. *(Jim Slosiarek/The Gazette)*

LEFT: Floodwater residue streaked the inside of McKinnon's Barber Shop on Ellis Boulevard and O Avenue in northwest Cedar Rapids. Photographed Tuesday, June 17. *(Courtney Sargent/The Gazette)*

BELOW: A refrigerator landed on the edge of a stream running through Ellis Park after floodwater receded in Cedar Rapids. Photographed Monday, June 16. *(Courtney Sargent/The Gazette)*

OPPOSITE PAGE: A row of houses near Bowling Street in southwest Cedar Rapids still was in a few feet of water on Saturday, June 14. *(Courtney Sargent/The Gazette)*

RIGHT: Michelle Horning (left) and her son, Stephen Horning, 16, on Tuesday, June 17, in their home of 13 years in southwest Cedar Rapids. The house took at least 5 feet of water. *(Courtney Sargent/The Gazette)*

BELOW: Striations on a packed car show the depth of floodwater in Cedar Rapids' Rompot neighborhood Saturday, June 14. *(Jim Slosiarek/The Gazette)*

OPPOSITE PAGE: Floodwater-stained clothes and other damaged items filled the Czech Village Salvation Army store in southwest Cedar Rapids when this photograph was taken Monday, June 16. *(Liz Martin/The Gazette)*

ABOVE: The CRANDIC railroad bridge over the Cedar River next to the Eighth Avenue bridge became a post-flood landmark after high water forced its collapse. Photographed Friday, June 27. *(Cliff Jette/The Gazette)*

LEFT: Artificial flowers in a glass jar were coated with silt in this Monday, June 16, photograph taken in Czech Village in southwest Cedar Rapids. *(Liz Martin/The Gazette)*

DOWNTOWN

*C*ruel irony was part of the cruelest summer in the history of downtown Cedar Rapids.

Several months before 2008 arrived, the city declared it the "Year of the River." City leaders secured private and public financing to rebuild the downtown area on both sides along the Cedar River and held special events downtown to try to lure new businesses and customers.

The Cedar was to be embraced as a focal point for downtown development. Among many goals in pumping up downtown were a park on both sides of the river and increased downtown housing.

The old goals were altered in June 2008 when a monstrous flood rendered much of downtown useless for a long time.

A dark skyline is never a good skyline for a city, but that's what Cedar Rapids had for several weeks after the flood. It didn't matter if you were a big bank or corner candy store. Your ground floor was gutted and you faced an overwhelming cleanup.

Water climbed 8 feet up the walls of The Garden Gate flower shop on Third Avenue SE.

"We imagined the worst," said shop owner Rebecca Pflughaupt, "and it was worse than that."

What made the devastation even harder to take was knowing downtown had been building a good buzz before the flood. Optimism for the future seemed justified. New restaurants had opened. Young adults had gravitated to downtown nightspots. Entrepreneurial companies had moved in, job numbers were growing, vacancies vanishing.

Renaissance shifted to recovery after the flood. Who would leave downtown for good? Who would start over there? How, and how soon?

A real and also symbolic sign of recovery came in early August when downtown icon Smulekoff's reopened its 118-year-old store on Third Avenue SE.

"I'm convinced that we will see a revitalized downtown come out of all this," Smulekoff's President Ann Lipsky said the week after the flooding.

It may take years to see if her forecast comes true. Maybe such early flickers of hope would lead to that skyline being fully lighted again one day.

The Gazette's front page,
Wednesday, June 18, 2008

OPPOSITE PAGE: Floodwaters surrounded the Linn County Courthouse and City Hall while covering May's Island in Cedar Rapids when the Cedar River crested on Friday, June 13. *(Liz Martin/The Gazette)*

OPPOSITE PAGE: Sandbags were in place to protect downtown Cedar Rapids businesses from potential flooding on Wednesday, June 11. The effort proved to be too little. *(Jim Slosiarek/The Gazette)*

ABOVE: By nightfall that day, the Cedar River was gaining on City Hall and May's Island. *(Jim Slosiarek/The Gazette)*

LEFT: People could walk on the First Avenue bridge near May's Island on Wednesday, June 11, but all the downtown Cedar Rapids bridges, except for Interstate 380, were closed to vehicular traffic. *(Jim Slosiarek/The Gazette)*

OPPOSITE PAGE: Guy Ayers-Berry and his crew needed a boat on Second Avenue SE when they searched for people waiting to be evacuated in Cedar Rapids on Thursday evening, June 12. Cedar Rapids police and Iowa National Guard troops had prohibited access to flooded parts of downtown. *(Jonathan D. Woods/The Gazette)*

LEFT: Debris-strewn floodwater from the Cedar River filled Second Avenue SE on Thursday, June 12. *(Cliff Jette/The Gazette)*

BELOW: The intersection of Third Street and Fourth Avenue SE around midday that day. *(Cliff Jette/The Gazette)*

OPPOSITE PAGE: Water over the Third Avenue bridge Thursday morning, June 12. *(Liz Martin/The Gazette)*

ABOVE: Smulekoff's windows were broken out and the store still had water at First Street and Third Avenue SE in downtown Cedar Rapids on Saturday, June 14. *(Cliff Jette/The Gazette)*

RIGHT: A bus took inmates across the flooded Third Avenue bridge after the Linn County Jail was evacuated Thursday morning, June 12. Some inmates and their families criticized the Sheriff's Office for waiting until then to move prisoners. *(Liz Martin/The Gazette)*

> *"Obviously, we didn't build the building anticipating it would be an aquarium."*
>
> Mercy Medical Center CEO Tim Charles, Friday, June 13

OPPOSITE PAGE: Cedar River floodwater surrounded the Quaker plant on Friday, June 13. *(Liz Martin/The Gazette)*

ABOVE: Police tried to keep Interstate 380 traffic flowing at midday Thursday, June 12. *(Cliff Jette/The Gazette)*

LEFT: Workers prepared to set up sump pumps Friday morning, June 13, in the lobby of Mercy Medical Center's Lundy Pavilion as the Cedar River neared its crest. *(Liz Martin/The Gazette)*

OPPOSITE PAGE: Employees, owners and volunteers gathered where the downtown skywalk starts, at the parking ramp adjacent to the U.S. Cellular Center, to salvage essential items at downtown businesses and organizations on Saturday, June 14. The city, Cedar Rapids Area Chamber of Commerce and Cedar Rapids Downtown District coordinated the effort, which was cut short to about a half-hour because of air quality concerns. Marion firefighters escorted people, who were not allowed into the flooded first floors. *(Cliff Jette/The Gazette)*

LEFT: Scott Wilcox, Cumulus Broadcasting chief engineer and technical director, removed servers from the Plaza 425 building that same day. *(Cliff Jette/The Gazette)*

BELOW LEFT: Gazette Communications receptionist Mary Ellen Johnson answered phones by lantern light at the company's downtown building on Thursday, June 12. The Gazette, GazetteOnline, KCRG-TV9 and kcrg.com had permission to stay in the flood zone to distribute emergency information. *(Cliff Jette/The Gazette)*

BELOW: Terry Weinacht, general manager of Cumulus Broadcasting, headed to his offices on the Plaza 425 building's fourth floor on Saturday, June 14. Cumulus operates KHAK-FM, KRNA-FM, KDAT-FM and KRQN-FM. *(Cliff Jette/The Gazette)*

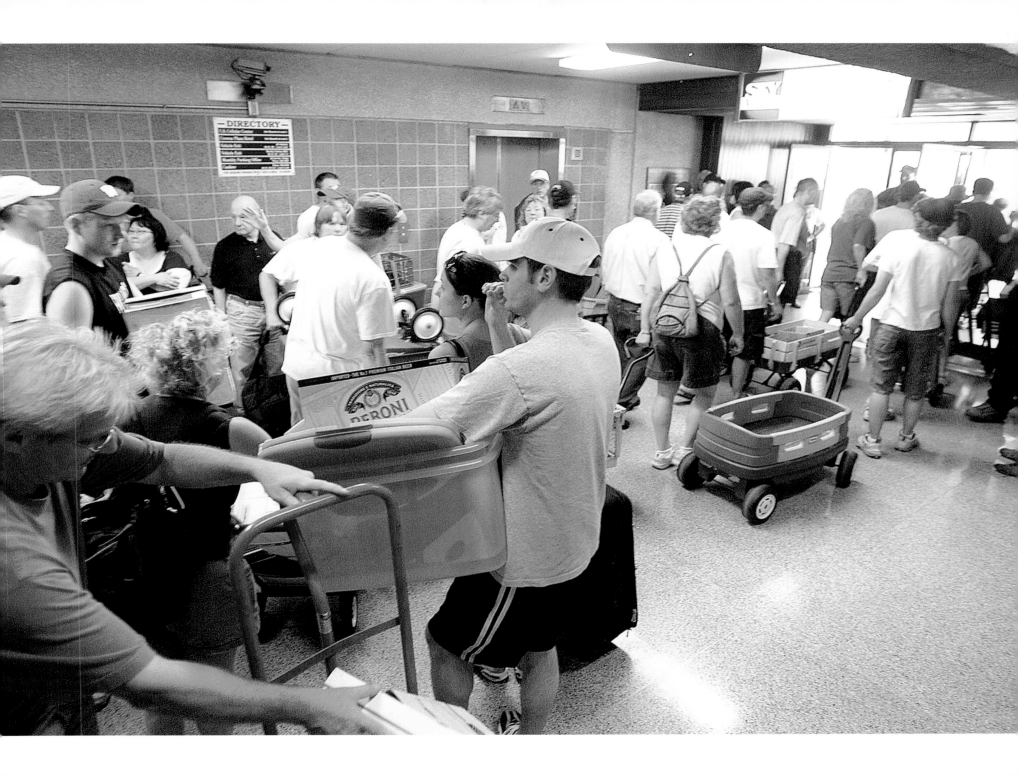

OPPOSITE PAGE: The flood knocked down the Paramount Theatre's front doors. Photographed Tuesday, June 17. *(Liz Martin/The Gazette)*

RIGHT: The Veterans Memorial window by Grant Wood at Cedar Rapids City Hall remained intact after floodwater receded. Photographed Tuesday, June 17. *(Liz Martin/The Gazette)*

BELOW: That same Tuesday, Cedar Rapids Public Library bookshelves were in disarray. The library sustained heavy damage. *(Liz Martin/The Gazette)*

OPPOSITE PAGE: A skid loader operator tore up the flood-damaged gymnasium floor when recovery efforts got under way at the Helen G. Nassif YMCA, 207 Seventh Ave. SE, on Thursday, June 19. *(Jonathan D. Woods/The Gazette)*

ABOVE: The YMCA's swimming pool was full of debris that Thursday. *(Jonathan D. Woods/The Gazette)*

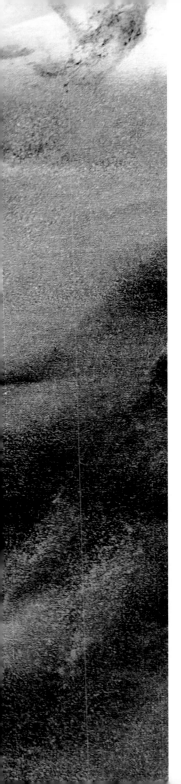

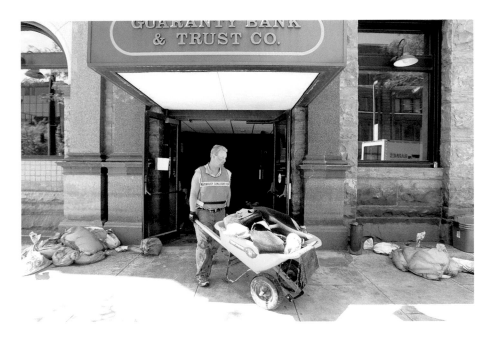

OPPOSITE PAGE: A tablecloth from Zins, 227 Second Ave. SE, showed evidence of a place setting that somehow remained on the table as floodwater overtook the restaurant. Photographed on Tuesday, June 17. *(Liz Martin/The Gazette)*

ABOVE: Volunteer Troy Shehan of Iowa City (right) carried a table out of the Piano Lounge in downtown Cedar Rapids on Tuesday, June 17, while lounge employee Ben Weber of Cedar Rapids searched for another. The lounge was in the basement. Waterlogged ceiling tiles and other debris created a deep swamplike muck on the floor. *(Liz Martin/The Gazette)*

LEFT: C.J. Eiben of Cedar Rapids hauled a wheelbarrow full of wet carpet out of Guaranty Bank and Trust, 302 Third Ave. SE, that Tuesday. *(Liz Martin/The Gazette)*

55

DOWNSTREAM

The National Acrobats of China, the Vienna Boys' Choir and "Monty Python's Spamalot" were among the scheduled offerings at Hancher Auditorium for its 2008-09 season.

In other words, it was to be a typical year in Iowa City as far as visits from world-renowned performers and productions. But then things got real atypical. There was a flood, and the world would stop coming to the University of Iowa via Hancher for at least a year.

Coralville Lake reached a record height, washed over its reservoir spillway and flowed downstream to the Iowa River. That pushed the river to a record level of 31.53 feet on June 15. Water entered 20 UI buildings, including Hancher, the 2,500-seat cultural jewel on the bank of the Iowa.

The first 15 rows of seats in Hancher's lower level were submerged.

Hancher's mechanical and electrical systems were damaged severely, rendering the auditorium unusable for performances for the entire school year. The cultural void joined the physical and financial losses that plagued the university and the Iowa City-Coralville area because of the flood.

This wasn't the area's first tango with a major flood.

It got pounded by one in 1993. But the 2008 version was worse, with 250 homes damaged in Iowa City's Normandy Drive/Parkview Terrace and Idyllwild neighborhoods. At least the UI had flood insurance for property loss. Coralville and Iowa City also had more of an idea of what to expect from their river than their Cedar Rapids neighbors to the north on Interstate 380. Coralville's longtime Edgewater Drive residents dealt with flooding in 1993.

Johnson County got hit hard.

More than 3 million sandbags were used in the county. Local government, residents, the university and its students came together to fill, tie, lift and stack the bags, trying to protect all they could. Some efforts were futile against the flood's force. Others did palpable good.

Much of the Coralville Strip was devastated by the flood. Inundated with mud and muck, business after business on that Highway 6 stretch stood closed after the deluge. Most were sidelined for months.

Meanwhile, some of Hancher's scheduled performances for 2008-09 were moved to other locations on campus and elsewhere in Iowa City. They, like the area, wouldn't quite be the same.

The Gazette's front page,
Friday, June 20, 2008

OPPOSITE PAGE: Lightning flashed in the sky when a storm front moved over the Coralville Lake emergency spillway at 2 a.m. Tuesday, June 10. It was a portent of things to come. Coralville Lake went over the spillway for only the second time in its 50-year history later that day. *(Brian Ray/The Gazette)*

OPPOSITE PAGE: Water rushed out of Coralville Lake's wide-open floodgates on Sunday afternoon, June 15. The man-made lake had crested at 5 a.m. that day at a record 716.97 feet above sea level. The old record from 1993 was 716.71 feet. *(Jonathan D. Woods/The Gazette)*

ABOVE: Alan Singleton pumped water from the area surrounding Bill and Susan Jones' home on Park Road near Rocky Shore Drive in Iowa City on Thursday, June 5. Only the basement had flooded at that time. The house took major floodwater later in June. *(Courtney Sargent/The Gazette)*

RIGHT: Water went over the Coralville Lake spillway June 10-24 into the Devonian Fossil Gorge. Photographed Sunday, June 22. *(Jonathan D. Woods/The Gazette)*

OPPOSITE PAGE: People came from around the area to sandbag the Iowa River along Iowa City's Normandy Drive on Monday, June 9. *(Jonathan D. Woods/The Gazette)*

LEFT: As the Iowa River's conditions deteriorated, Iowa City Mayor Regenia Bailey issued mandatory evacuation orders for residents along the river on Thursday, June 12. The Normandy Drive area was first, a little after midnight. Iowa City Police Investigator Mike Smithey (right) and Officer Abe Schabilion were among police going door to door when this photo was taken at 1:45 a.m. The river breached the levee there around 11 a.m. *(Brian Ray/The Gazette)*

BELOW: Dave Patton of North Liberty floated out the last two rubber totes of his parents' possessions from their Normandy Drive home on Thursday, June 12. *(Brian Ray/The Gazette)*

61

OPPOSITE PAGE TOP LEFT: Covered with mud, Iowa National Guard Staff Sgt. Tonya Wegner could smile during the Baculis Mobile Home Park sandbagging operation Monday, June 16. *(Jonathan D. Woods/The Gazette)*

OPPOSITE PAGE BOTTOM LEFT: Walking on pallets to avoid sinking into the extremely soft ground, Iowa National Guard troops unloaded sandbags to reinforce a levee at Baculis Mobile Home Park in Iowa City that same Monday. The crew worked several hours to boost the levee's integrity. *(Jonathan D. Woods/The Gazette)*

OPPOSITE PAGE RIGHT: Inside the University of Iowa Main Library, volunteers passed some of the library's 500,000 books in basement storage on Friday, June 13. Kristi Bontrager, the University Libraries public relations coordinator, said the irreplaceable Special Collections Department items had been moved to higher ground earlier in the week. *(Brian Ray/The Gazette)*

RIGHT: Hundreds of volunteers responded to a call to fill sandbags along Madison Street at the University of Iowa on Saturday, June 14, as the rising Iowa River flooded the campus. *(Brian Ray/The Gazette)*

"We've never seen a threat like this before."

University of Iowa President Sally Mason, Saturday, June 14

LEFT: The Coralville Strip, which is Highway 6, was under water in this Monday, June 16, photo looking toward the southwest toward Iowa City. *(Brian Ray/The Gazette)*

ABOVE: Wig and Pen owner Dick Querrey tried to close a window after checking his business on Friday, June 20, on the Coralville Strip. *(Brian Ray/The Gazette)*

OPPOSITE PAGE TOP: Old Chicago co-owner Joe McLaughlin addressed his employees as they left the Coralville Strip restaurant for the last time while floodwater surrounded the restaurant on Thursday, June 12. *(Brian Ray/The Gazette)*

OPPOSITE PAGE BOTTOM: At another part of the city, Marine One flew President Bush over the Coralville Marriott Hotel & Conference Center when the president viewed flood zones in Cedar Rapids, Coralville and Iowa City on Thursday, June 19. *(Liz Martin/The Gazette)*

"Sometimes you get dealt a hand you didn't expect to have to play. It's not a question whether you're going to play it. The question is how you're going to play it. I'm confident the people of Iowa will play it well."

President Bush, during trip to Cedar Rapids and Iowa City, Thursday, June 19

OPPOSITE PAGE: Floodwater covered Dubuque Street near the Park Road Bridge in Iowa City in this Tuesday, June 10, photograph. The water eventually rose past Dubuque Street's intersection with Park Road and over the bridge. *(Brian Ray/The Gazette)*

TOP LEFT: Matt McCarter, a University of Iowa junior from Willow Springs, Ill. (left), and Kelen Eddy, a spring UI graduate from Coal City, Ill., filled sandbags in front of the Clapp Recital Hall in Iowa City on Tuesday, June 10, in a bid to protect the UI Arts Campus from the rising Iowa River. *(Liz Martin/ The Gazette)*

BOTTOM LEFT: The river won the battle. Water still was in Hancher Auditorium's first few rows when UI Building and Landscape Services engineer Elson Byler led a media tour of the building on Thursday, June 19. *(Brian Ray/The Gazette)*

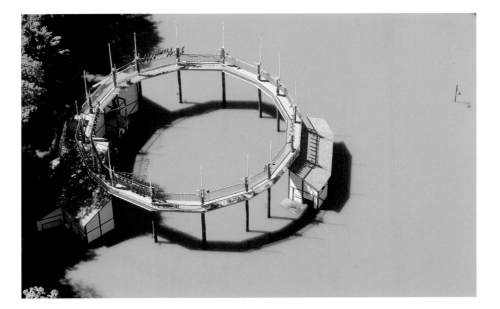

OPPOSITE PAGE: Only the top of the Iowa City's landmark City Park merry-go-round was visible above the Iowa River floodwater in this photo, taken Friday, June 13. *(Liz Martin/The Gazette)*

ABOVE: Floodwater surrounded Iowa City's sewage treatment facility along the Iowa River north of Highway 6 on Friday, June 13. *(Liz Martin/The Gazette)*

LEFT: Flooding covered the Riverside Theatre Festival Stage's seats and stage at City Park in Iowa City. Photographed on Monday, June 16. *(Brian Ray/The Gazette)*

OPPOSITE PAGE: This view looking north shows the extent of flooding businesses contended with along South Gilbert Street and Stevens Drive in southern Iowa City. Photograph taken on Monday, June 16. *(Brian Ray/The Gazette)*

ABOVE: Dale Simon in the living room of his home in Iowa City's Idyllwild neighborhood on Saturday, June 21. Simon, who moved most of his furniture out before the flood, took about 3 feet of floodwater in his home. *(Brian Ray/ The Gazette)*

RIGHT: Church administrator Jim Douglass opened windows so moist air could escape from Parkview Evangelical Free Church, on Foster Road near Dubuque Street in Iowa City. The church campus sustained heavy flooding damage. Photograph taken on Friday, June 20. *(Jonathan D. Woods/The Gazette)*

DISRUPTION

It wasn't always called Czech Village, but it always was the Czech village.

It encompassed parts of the southeast and southwest sides of the Cedar River in Cedar Rapids. Starting in the 19th century, immigrants from Czechoslovakia settled there. They opened businesses, many of them connected as much to their old world as their new one.

The eastern end of 16th Avenue SW was a vital commercial and residential area for more than a century. Polehna's Meat Market, for example, sold Czech meats in the same location since 1931.

But Polehna's got knocked out of business by the floods of 2008. So did everything else in Czech Village.

"There's a lot of people worse off from me," Polehna's owner Mike Ferguson said the week after the flood. "But I lost my future."

Czech Village and other flood-devastated neighborhoods in Cedar Rapids and Eastern Iowa had iffy futures. Decisions on whether to rebuild were difficult for some. For others it was no decision at all. It was simply going to be done. Or, it simply wasn't.

The Time Check area in northwest Cedar Rapids was walloped and destined to change dramatically. While some in the area vowed to rebuild, it seemed certain bulldozers eventually would be as present there as sludge the river left behind.

Many of the homeowners in the Rompot/Cedar Valley neighborhood on the city's southeast side had paid off their houses. That offered little consolation when they were displaced by the flood. As in Czech Village and Time Check, many of the residents were unsure if or how they would return.

While remaining the same size physically, Cedar Rapids seemed to be shrinking. The prospect of the city without certain longtime neighborhoods was hard to fathom.

The National Czech & Slovak Museum & Library in Czech Village opened in 1995, with a dedication ceremony that brought together the presidents of the United States, the Czech Republic and Slovakia. The building had up to 10 feet of floodwater inside, but will be renovated.

What kind of neighborhood the museum would be part of after it reopened was a question without a clear answer.

The Gazette's front page,
Monday, June 16, 2008

OPPOSITE PAGE: Alice Galvin was walking on Fifth Street NW toward her Time Check neighborhood home in northwest Cedar Rapids when this photograph was taken Friday, June 27. Her home was damaged badly in the flood of 1993. This time, she said, her family would not rebuild. *(Liz Martin/The Gazette)*

OPPOSITE PAGE: The Time Check neighborhood in northwest Cedar Rapids, at its worst. *(Brian Ray/The Gazette)*

ABOVE: Sheila Goad (left) took comfort from her sister, Deb Bute of Cedar Rapids, after one of Goad's pets was found dead in her Time Check home on Friday, June 20. Goad and another sister, Shawn Crippen, lived in the home together and left behind five pets in the mandatory evacuation. *(Liz Martin/The Gazette)*

LEFT: Josh Clemann (center) handed Justin Danford a box while Clemann's wife, Jennifer Clemann, watched from the second-story window as the three cleaned the second story of the Clemanns' Time Check home on Friday, June 20. Danford, who is Jennifer Clemann's ex-husband, also had flood damage to his northwest Cedar Rapids home. *(Liz Martin/The Gazette)*

OPPOSITE PAGE: Hundreds of residents anxiously waited Sunday, June 15, at a checkpoint on Bowling Street SW and 21st Avenue to get into their homes after floodwater receded in southwest Cedar Rapids. *(Courtney Sargent/The Gazette)*

ABOVE: Vince Fiala (left) became the face of Cedar Rapids homeowners' frustration on Sunday, June 15, when he confronted a police officer about not having access to his southwest Cedar Rapids home. His daughter, Diane Stanek, clutched his arm outside a checkpoint on Bowling Street and 21st Avenue SW. A strike team had not yet declared any homes in the area safe for residents to enter, and tension quickly rose. *(Courtney Sargent/The Gazette)*

RIGHT: Air National Guard Senior Airman Katie Grenier of Sioux City directed a vehicle around the intersection of 16th Avenue and Sixth Street SW in Cedar Rapids on Thursday, June 12, after flooding closed 16th Avenue. *(Liz Martin/The Gazette)*

77

OPPOSITE PAGE: The National Czech & Slovak Museum & Library, 30 16th Ave. SW, another Cedar Rapids landmark the flood overtook. Photographed on Friday, June 13. *(Liz Martin/The Gazette)*

ABOVE: Volunteer Bob Drahozal of Cedar Rapids (far left) and librarian David Muhlena removed a piece of artwork from the National Czech & Slovak Museum & Library when employees and volunteers began salvaging museum artifacts on Tuesday, June 17. A refrigerated semitrailer truck stored the flood-damaged books until attempts to restore them could start. *(Cliff Jette/The Gazette)*

LEFT: Czech Village, including the museum in the background, emerged from the flood on Monday, June 16. *(Brian Ray/The Gazette)*

OPPOSITE PAGE: Urban Search and Rescue team member and Cedar Rapids firefighter Eric Vandewater of North Liberty was among those checking Czech Village homes for flood damage. In this photo, taken Monday, June 16, he is with Talyn, a search and rescue dog. Teams forced entry into homes when safety could not be determined from outside. *(Liz Martin/The Gazette)*

TOP RIGHT: Barb Ferguson, wife of the owner of Polehna's Meat Market, received a hug from state Rep. Art Staed, D-Cedar Rapids, while waiting outside the flood-ravaged business on 16th Avenue in Czech Village on Tuesday, June 17. The Fergusons decided in late summer to close Polehna's instead of rebuilding. *(Cliff Jette/The Gazette)*

BOTTOM RIGHT: High water delivered heavy damage to homes like this one near Bowling Street in southwest Cedar Rapids, photographed on Saturday, June 14. *(Courtney Sargent/The Gazette)*

OPPOSITE PAGE: Volunteers from Des Moines and Minneapolis helped local residents remove holy books, cassettes and historic documents from Mother Mosque of America, 1335 Ninth St. NW, in Cedar Rapids on Saturday, June 21. *(Jonathan D. Woods/The Gazette)*

ABOVE: Boathouses in the Ellis Park Harbor were tipped from their moorings on Thursday, June 12, when this photo was taken in Cedar Rapids. *(Jim Slosiarek/The Gazette)*

LEFT: Henry Davison was on the telephone in front of his flood-damaged H.D. Youth Center, 1006 Third St. SE, on Thursday, June 19, calling volunteers to help clean the center. *(Jim Slosiarek/The Gazette)*

> *"It won't be the same ever again. ... But hey, I'm not the only one, right?"*
>
> Manager Jeff Melsha, Little Bohemia tavern, 1317 Third St. SE, Cedar Rapids, on Monday, June 23

OPPOSITE PAGE: Little Bohemia was reflected in floodwater at the intersection of 14th Avenue and Third Street SE in Cedar Rapids when the sun rose Wednesday, June 11. *(Liz Martin/The Gazette)*

ABOVE: The flooded part of St. Patrick's Church, 510 First Ave. NW, in Cedar Rapids on Friday, June 13. *(Cliff Jette/The Gazette)*

LEFT: Another Cedar Rapids landmark, the Dairy Queen at 208 First Ave. NW, was almost submerged on Thursday, June 12. It, too, became one of the Cedar's victims when the post-flood decision was made to demolish it. *(Courtney Sargent/The Gazette)*

OPPOSITE PAGE: Volunteer Candace Chihak (left) of Lisbon had to break through the wall of Gloria Ruzicka's kitchen while other volunteers helped remove the flood-damaged drywall in Ruzicka's southwest Cedar Rapids home on Saturday, June 28. Ruzicka, who is disabled, called for help from volunteers. *(Courtney Sargent/The Gazette)*

RIGHT: A wayward clown nose came to rest with remaining water and silt at Balloons Etc., 720 Center Point Rd. NE, in Cedar Rapids on Wednesday, June 18. Owners Kimberly and Jacob Cowger cleaned and salvaged what they could so they could operate the business out of their Marion home. Jacob performs as Sparkles the Clown. *(Cliff Jette/The Gazette)*

BELOW: Cribs and other contents were outside Building Blocks Child Care, 350 Third Ave. SW, on Thursday, June 19. *(Jonathan D. Woods/The Gazette)*

DESTINATION

If you threw a dart at a map of Iowa in June 2008, it probably made a splash.

The floods didn't belong only to Cedar Rapids or Iowa City. Eighty-five of Iowa's 99 counties received presidential disaster declarations because of flood damage.

Palo, seven miles from Cedar Rapids, was evacuated the week of the flooding. National Guard Humvees blocked entrances into town. Rare was the building in the town unharmed by the Cedar River.

A week after the flood, Betty Thompson of Palo said she lost everything except some clothes. "It is just a day-by-day process," she said. "We can't do any more than that."

The Cedar crested at 24.7 feet in Vinton, more than 5 feet above the previous record there. The town went without electricity for two days. Sections of Highway 150, the main artery into Vinton, were closed north of town.

During the week of the flood, a doctor who lived north of Vinton had to make a 75-mile drive to get from his home to his Vinton office.

About $20 million worth of damage was incurred. The Benton County Law Enforcement Center was rendered unusable in Vinton. The Sheriff's Office relocated in a former elementary school.

Elkader is a picturesque community in northeast Iowa. It was named Iowa River Town of the Year in April by Iowa Rivers Revival, a non-profit organization. Fishing and canoeing the Turkey River are popular among its residents and guests.

But the Turkey turned wild in early June, cresting in Elkader at a record 30.9 feet. A blacktop playground was among many things that floated down the Turkey during the flood.

Anamosa's wastewater treatment plant suffered $3 million worth of harm thanks to the flooded Wapsipinicon River. The Wapsie also severely damaged homes in Olin.

In Decorah, the Upper Iowa River flooded parts of Luther College's lower campus. It was the town's worst flood in at least a half-century.

Manchester and Dorchester. Columbus Junction and Oxford Junction. They and too many other Iowa towns endured destruction from floods.

The names of the rivers changed from area to area, but the sad stories many left behind were similar.

The Gazette's front page,
Thursday, June 12, 2008

OPPOSITE PAGE: Shirts hanging in Penney Courtney and Britt Meister's home in Vinton were soiled by floodwater that ravaged the home in June. Photographed Sunday, June 15. *(Angela Holmes/The Gazette)*

> *"Do what you can while you can.*
> *And if you can't, it's too late."*
>
> Vinton resident Becky Hessenius, Tuesday, June 10

OPPOSITE PAGE: The Iowa River spread wide upstream from Marengo in Iowa County on Wednesday, June 11. The river flows into the man-made Coralville Lake in Johnson County. *(Cliff Jette/The Gazette)*

ABOVE: Floodwater rose into southeast Palo on Wednesday, June 11. *(Cliff Jette/The Gazette)*

RIGHT: Floodwater from the Cedar River inundated Vinton that same Wednesday. *(Cliff Jette/The Gazette)*

OPPOSITE PAGE: Linda Urban of Vinton was rescued by her son, Dan Adams (left), and Richard VanFosson after floodwater reached her Vinton home on Wednesday, June 11. *(Courtney Sargent/The Gazette)*

LEFT: Iowa National Guard soldiers built a sandbag wall around the Benton County Law Enforcement Center that day. *(Courtney Sargent/The Gazette)*

BELOW: Benton County Jail inmates were evacuated by boat in Vinton on Wednesday, June 11. *(Courtney Sargent/The Gazette)*

OPPOSITE PAGE: Jacob Hessenius, 15, (left) and Paul Walker, 16, of Vinton carried possessions out of Jeff and Rhonda Sojka's home as rain pummeled Vinton on Wednesday, June 11. *(Courtney Sargent/The Gazette)*

ABOVE: Nicole Williams, (left to right) Tim Newnaber and Kevin Berry waited for a boat to pick them up from the front yard of Newnaber's parents' Vinton home on Thursday, June 12. *(Courtney Sargent/The Gazette)*

RIGHT: Brian Geiger (left) of Van Horne and Lois Kray of Vinton checked damage at a friend's home in Vinton that same Thursday. *(Courtney Sargent/The Gazette)*

"*When I got the call last night I was in tears because my whole childhood is in this house.*"

Debbie Langguth of Cedar Rapids, Tuesday, June 10

OPPOSITE PAGE: Volunteers stockpiled sand-bags at the Palo Community Center on Tuesday, June 10, as they prepared for more flooding along the Cedar River. *(Cliff Jette/The Gazette)*

ABOVE: After floodwater receded, volunteers helped Philip Hughes (left) clean up the Lincoln Drive home where he and his wife, Joanna Hughes, live in Palo. Photographed Friday, June 27. *(Jonathan D. Woods/The Gazette)*

LEFT: Debbie Langguth of Cedar Rapids helped her father, George Shakespeare, remove items from his home when Palo prepared for flooding on Tuesday, June 10. George and Mary Shake-speare have lived in their Lincoln Drive home for 35 years. *(Cliff Jette/The Gazette)*

97

OPPOSITE PAGE: Floodwater from the burgeoned Iowa River threatened levees in Columbus Junction on Saturday afternoon, June 14. *(Jonathan D. Woods/ The Gazette)*

ABOVE: Columbus Junction residents trying to reinforce a railway line with sandbags were forced to retreat after floodwater collapsed the levee that Saturday. Spirits sank as an evacuation was ordered. *(Jonathan D. Woods/The Gazette)*

LEFT: A bouquet of artificial flowers and caution tape marked where the 110-year-old Sutliff Bridge crossed the Cedar River in northeast Johnson County before the flood dislodged it. Photographed Saturday, July 12. *(Rollin Banderob/The Gazette)*

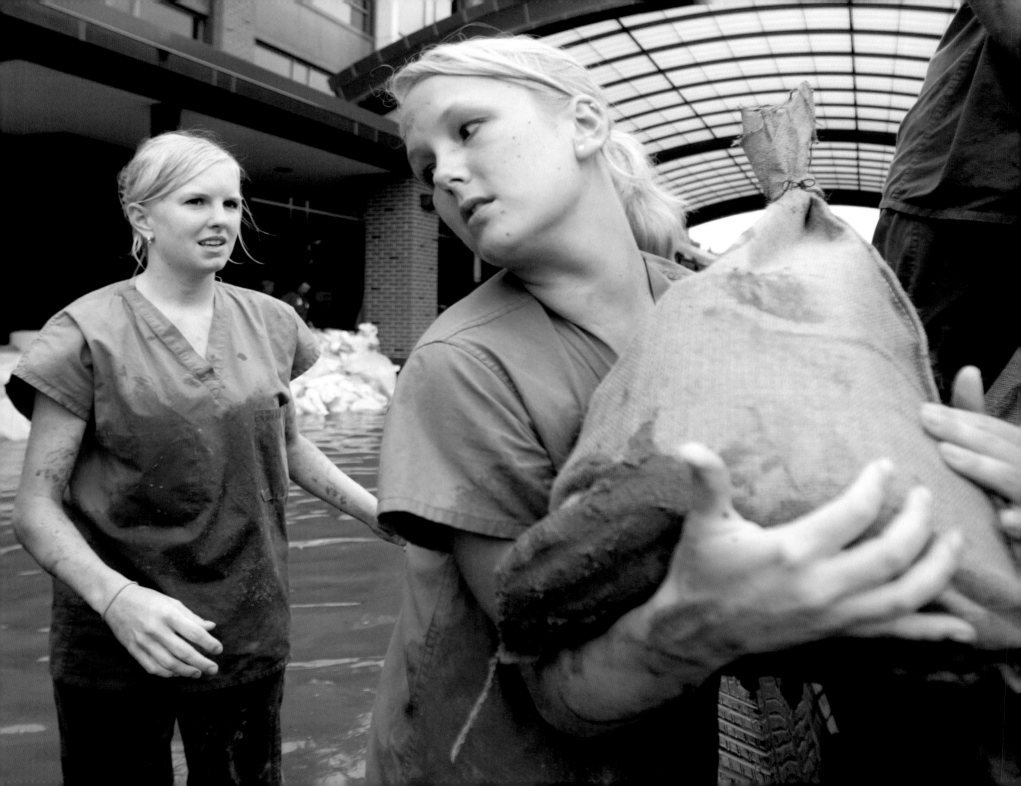

DETERMINATION

*I*t was 1,200 people hurriedly assembling late at night on Edgewood Road NW in Cedar Rapids for sandbagging.

They saved Collector Well 3 and the city's water supply. What if they hadn't heeded a call for help on local television and radio?

But it was also one person — one of thousands — using weekends or personal vacation time to help clear the mud and muck from someone else's home.

Determination. Without it, the flood-clobbered cities of Eastern Iowa might as well have put up "Closed" signs at their city limits.

It was the staffs of the Salvation Army and American Red Cross working day after day, week after week, to provide food, supplies and shelter to those affected by flooding.

It was neighbors, friends and family members helping the afflicted in countless ways.

It was brigades of people from well beyond Iowa seeing a region hit by a natural disaster and bringing help. Why did they come? Because it was needed.

It was sleep-deprived employees of Eastern Iowa cities and counties doing vital work. It was also citizens, musclemen and schoolgirls. It was people opening their homes to someone else who was suddenly without one.

Most of all, it was the flood victims themselves not caving in to their plights, but putting their brains and brawn to use in figuring out ways to survive and proceed through terrible times. "One day at a time" never felt more meaningful.

Long after the adrenaline rush of fighting the flood and its aftermath had passed, people dug in for the thankless dirty work of cleaning up.

Everyone in the area, it seemed, had a story about someone else's generosity or resolve. Many whose homes or businesses got battered by flooding still made time to assist someone else. Those who faced nature's amazing power countered with a strength of their own. Every ounce of it mattered.

Ten thousand sandbags surrounded and preserved Collector Well 3 that June 12 night. Cedar Rapids' water supply was saved. Who knows what the fallout would have been had all those volunteers not shown up so quickly. And so determinedly.

The Gazette's front page, Thursday, June 19, 2008

OPPOSITE PAGE: Cardiovascular-interventional radiographer Amber Holst (left) and nurse Tracy Neurohr were part of the sandbagging effort at the front entrance of Mercy Medical Center in Cedar Rapids on Thursday afternoon, June 12. *(Jonathan D. Woods/The Gazette)*

OPPOSITE PAGE: Volunteers formed a human chain on Friday, June 13, to carry sandbags at Mercy Medical Center in southeast Cedar Rapids. *(Jim Slosiarek/The Gazette)*

ABOVE: Gov. Chet Culver thanked volunteers filling sandbags at the Palo Community Center on Tuesday, June 10. The governor made several visits to flooded Eastern Iowa in June. *(Cliff Jette/The Gazette)*

LEFT: Oliver Chalkley, 9, of Iowa City grabbed a sandbag from a fellow volunteer in the backyard of a home on Iowa City's Normandy Drive on Saturday, June 7. *(Courtney Sargent/The Gazette)*

OPPOSITE PAGE: Cedar Rapids firefighter Brent Smith (left) and Brandon Adams (right) helped Louie Moran of Cedar Rapids walk to safety on First Avenue after being rescued from his home at 814 Third Ave. SW in Cedar Rapids on Thursday evening, June 12. *(Jonathan D. Woods/The Gazette)*

LEFT: Briar Patterson, 15, and his father, Duane Patterson, both of Cedar Rapids, navigated the floodwater on O Avenue NW between Eighth and Ninth streets with a friend's refrigerator aboard their boat on Thursday, June 12. *(Liz Martin/The Gazette)*

BELOW: Beo Hoang, a Normandy Drive resident in Iowa City, walked through floodwater with her son, Keo, after the truck she was being evacuated in stalled on Thursday, June 12. *(Brian Ray/The Gazette)*

OPPOSITE PAGE: Volunteers sandbagged Cedar Rapids' only remaining well, then made and loaded sandbags for Mercy Medical Center the night of Thursday, June 12. Some 1,200 men, women and children converged on the south end of the Edgewood Road bridge, where the well exists. *(Jim Slosiarek/The Gazette)*

ABOVE: Many of the volunteers sandbagging Collector Well 3 worked late into the night. *(Jim Slosiarek/The Gazette)*

LEFT: Tiffin volunteer firefighters Jack Eggers (left) and Ray Forman (right) helped Karen Spieker out of a boat and to her wheelchair Friday, June 13, as floodwater from Clear Creek covered Highway 6 in Coralville. Spieker and her husband, Frank, had to be evacuated from their Coralville apartment after high water prevented their son from getting them. *(Brian Ray/The Gazette)*

OPPOSITE PAGE: University of Iowa graduates Regan and Aurelia Mena, from Austin, Texas, didn't let the flood change their wedding day; it just changed their plans on Saturday, June 14, in Iowa City. The Menas were to exchange vows on the Iowa Memorial Union terrace and have a reception at Kinnick Stadium. But flooding overtook the terrace. So they exchanged vows at the Englert Theatre in downtown Iowa City. They walked to the floodwater to have their photo taken. *(Brian Ray/The Gazette)*

LEFT: Members of Iowa City's Parkview Evangelical Church moved their worship services to West High School on Sunday, June 15. Despite sandbagging, floodwater from the Iowa River overtook the church's campus at 15 Foster Rd. *(Jonathan D. Woods/The Gazette)*

BELOW: Judy Polumbaum retrieved some belongings and inspected her home on Park Place, near Normandy Drive, in Iowa City. Floodwater was receding, but standing water still was in dozens of homes in that neighborhood when this photograph was taken on Tuesday, June 17. *(Jonathan D. Woods/The Gazette)*

OPPOSITE PAGE: Bonnie Dean of the Humane Society of Missouri counted pet rats in cages trapped in a Cedar Rapids apartment on First Street and Sixth Avenue SW while her colleagues searched a bedroom for 11 cats also living in the apartment. Photographed on Saturday, June 14. *(Courtney Sargent/The Gazette)*

RIGHT: Chris Davidson of the Navy (left), Dan Ripley of the Cedar Rapids Fire Department (second from left) and Brian Collingsworth of the Navy (right) pushed a rescue boat down First Street SW carrying the 11 cats, 18 rats and two birds they rescued from a southwest Cedar Rapids home on Saturday, June 14. *(Courtney Sargent/The Gazette)*

BELOW: Jeff Palmer (left) of Cedar Rapids handed Lauri Haldeman, also of Cedar Rapids, Gene Minder's dog after Cedar Rapids and Ely firefighters rescued it from Minder's Ellis Boulevard NW home. Water rose to nearly 6 feet in his living room Thursday, June 12. *(Liz Martin/ The Gazette)*

OPPOSITE PAGE: Coralville Fire Department Assistant Chiefs Orey Schwitzer (left) and Bill Horning (center) took Mayor Jim Fausett (right) on a boat tour down Coralville's First Avenue as the Iowa River crested on Sunday, June 15. *(Jonathan D. Woods/The Gazette)*

ABOVE: Volunteers from Serve The City distributed free water given by the Federal Emergency Management Agency when Cedar Rapids was conserving its scarce water supply. Volunteer Donovan Jones (left), 10, of Robins handed a package of water bottles to volunteer Stacie Wiley of Marion for distribution in this photograph, taken Sunday, June 15. *(Courtney Sargent/The Gazette)*

RIGHT: Staff Sgt. Layne Marti, of the 211th General Support Aviation Battalion, unhooked a motor retrieved from a non-functioning water pump at Cedar Rapids' J Avenue Water Treatment Plant on Monday, June 16. Three sets of pumps were out of service at the facility. *(Courtney Sargent/The Gazette)*

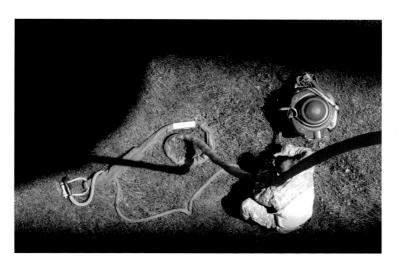

OPPOSITE PAGE: Liz Mathis, vice president of community relations for Horizons in Cedar Rapids, was working out of her car in a parking lot in northeast Cedar Rapids on Monday, July 14. She used a laptop and cell phone, plus files and office supplies packed into her trunk, as she traveled to where the family resource agency was working in the Cedar Rapids metro area. *(Jim Slosiarek/The Gazette)*

RIGHT: Iowa City Mayor Regenia Bailey gave President Bush an update on local flood damage during a briefing at Kirkwood Community College in Cedar Rapids on Thursday, June 19. Listening was Iowa Gov. Chet Culver. *(Liz Martin/The Gazette)*

BELOW: Cedar Rapids Mayor Kay Halloran and council member Brian Fagan on Wednesday, June 18, during the City Council's first meeting after the flood. The council met at a temporary location at The Eastern Iowa Airport. *(Liz Martin/The Gazette)*

OPPOSITE PAGE: Minnesota Vikings linebacker and former University of Iowa football player Chad Greenway (left) picked up flood debris with a fan, Caleb Crossett (right), 9, of Coralville in City Park in Iowa City on Friday, July 18. *(Courtney Sargent/The Gazette)*

LEFT: Employee Emily Daliensen carries trash out of Mondo's Tomato Pie during flood cleanup along Highway 6 in Coralville on Thursday, June 19. *(Brian Ray/The Gazette)*

ABOVE: Mount Vernon firefighter Dan Gines took a needed break after launching a boat to recover a Cedar Rapids resident trapped on a rooftop on Thursday evening, June 12. *(Jonathan D. Woods/The Gazette)*

DISCOVERY

*F*iscal, physical and psychological tolls the floods of 2008 took on Eastern Iowa will be felt for a long time, and that's a fact.

But while the disaster brought no good, much goodness was witnessed during and after the flooding.

Cedar Rapids, Coralville and other flood-pounded cities throughout the area seemed unwilling to surrender and crumble. The region fell off national newscasts once floodwaters receded, perhaps because its people quietly and quickly started rebuilding rather than infighting.

Crime sprees during the flood and those first days immediately following it? Nonexistent. People taking care of other people and trying to take care of themselves? Omnipresent.

Whenever you passed through a stricken area in the months after the flooding, you inevitably saw someone pushing forward.

"When that guy up the street comes out of his house with another wheelbarrow, the city takes another micro-step," said Dennis Hill of Cedar Rapids, who bought and began rebuilding a house on the city's Ellis Boulevard NW after the flood.

"As long as you look at it that way, there's hope for Ellis and hope for everybody. It's just baby steps. Sometimes you step on nails, but they're steps."

New Yorker Ira Goldman ran an American Red Cross shelter at Viola Gibson Elementary School in Cedar Rapids for people displaced by the flood. It wasn't his first disaster-site assignment, but he sure made it sound like it was his best.

"I've never seen anything like Cedar Rapids," Goldman said. "I'm not even sure I'm joking when I say if the hurricane they're preparing for in New York ever happens and I have to evacuate, I'm coming to Cedar Rapids. Because the people here take care of each other. People keep telling me it's an Iowa thing."

Maybe it is an Iowa thing. The easy thing for many people would have been to walk away from their houses rather than try to rebuild them. Some did make that choice, many because they lacked the resources to begin again. But many dug in for the slow, smelly, dirty, lousy job of cleaning out and starting over.

When asked why, their answers never seemed to vary much. This is home.

The Gazette's front page, Saturday, July 12, 2008

OPPOSITE PAGE: Recovery Construction Services workers Scott Yanda (left) and Jeff Middleton, both of Cedar Rapids, hauled damaged appliances out of Smulekoff's, 97 Third Ave. SE, along the Cedar River on Friday, June 20. The longtime downtown fixture reopened Saturday, Aug. 2. *(Jim Slosiarek/The Gazette)*

The Cedar River doing its worst on Thursday, June 12 (above), and back below the record flood level on July 9 (opposite page). *(Liz Martin/The Gazette)*

121

ABOVE: Iowa City firefighters Tina McDermott and Darrall Brick used a rubber boat to evacuate Paul Measells from Measells' Normandy Drive home in Iowa City on Thursday, June 12. Measells was unable to walk out of the area because of a medical condition. *(Brian Ray/The Gazette)*

OPPOSITE PAGE: Scott Anderson waved to a passing car as he washed his driveway at the same site on Normandy Drive on Wednesday, July 9. *(Liz Martin/The Gazette)*

> *"We were building a home together."*
>
> Julie Stevens, Cedar Rapids, on June 29

OPPOSITE PAGE: Todd Gareau and his fiancee, Julie Stevens, had lived in a renovated home they wanted to buy at 301 I Ave. NW for six months when the flood hit. When they were photographed Sunday, June 29, with their dog, Jack, the couple said they wanted to leave Iowa. *(Liz Martin/The Gazette)*

ABOVE: Paul Solar and his dog Cleo on the front steps of their home at 1807 First St. SW in Cedar Rapids. The home was tabbed for demolition because of significant damage to its foundation. Solar had lived in the 100-year-old house, which he owned, for nine months before the flood forced him to evacuate. Photographed on Wednesday, Aug. 6. *(Cliff Jette/The Gazette)*

LEFT: Michael Richards and his wife, Liza Duquilla, in front of their flood-ravaged home at 1019 Third St. SE in Cedar Rapids' New Bohemia neighborhood on Sunday, June 29. The couple lived in the house, the Vavra House, which is part of the National Trust for Historic Preservation district on Third Street SE, for five years before the flood hit. *(Cliff Jette/The Gazette)*

OPPOSITE PAGE: Brian and Angie West (back left and center) owned at house at 831 G Ave. NW and rented it to Angie's sisters, Lucinda Schmeiser (back right) and Lori Schmeiser (not pictured). In this Tuesday, July 1, photograph are Angie's children, Ryanna Sliter, 12 (front left) and Andrew Sliter, 7. The Schmeiser sisters had lived in the house for about a year before the flood struck. The flood took most of their possessions, but a desk Angie's and Lucinda's grandfather made remained. *(Liz Martin/The Gazette)*

LEFT: Jerry Bemer lived at 1223 Fourth St. NW for 10 years. The water reached above the roof line and knocked the house off its foundation, but Bemer planned to stay in Cedar Rapids. Photographed Thursday, July 10. *(Liz Martin/The Gazette)*

OPPOSITE PAGE: Smulekoff's employee Geri Emig (left) gave Smulekoff's President Ann Lipsky a handful of jewelry, some possibly belonging to Lipsky's father, that was recovered from the store at 97 Third Ave. SE on Friday, June 20. *(Jim Slosiarek/The Gazette)*

LEFT: Susan Stamats of Cedar Rapids (left) watched as Guaranty Bank Senior Vice President Chris Crosby of Cedar Rapids opened Stamats' safe-deposit box at the bank in downtown Cedar Rapids, 302 Third Ave. SE, on Tuesday, June 24. *(Liz Martin/The Gazette)*

BELOW: Thomas Meade of rural Stone City carefully opened the abstract for his home at Guaranty Bank with help from Ron Davis of Rushville, N.Y., a project manager for Document Reprocessors. Guaranty safe-deposit box customers were allowed on June 24 to retrieve their boxes from the flooded vault, clean the contents and send important documents to a restorer. *(Liz Martin/The Gazette)*

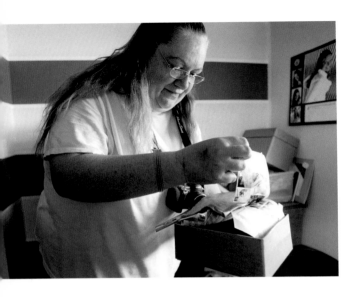

OPPOSITE PAGE: New Hexagonaria coral fossils emerged at Coralville Lake's Devonian Fossil Gorge after water stopped pouring over the lake's nearby spillway. Photographed on Sunday, June 22, two days before water stopped going over the spillway. *(Jonathan D. Woods/The Gazette)*

ABOVE: Mary Dickinson looked through her daughter's photos after floodwater receded enough at Dickinson's Time Check neighborhood home on 10th Street NW for her to safely enter on Sunday, June 15. Dickinson had stored her important property up high before evacuating, but some items fell to the floor and were ruined. *(Courtney Sargent/ The Gazette)*

RIGHT: Sheila Chase took her five cats to a shelter at Kirkwood Community College's Iowa Equestrian Center after being evacuated from her southwest Cedar Rapids home during the flood. Photographed with her cat Millie on Friday, June 20. *(Courtney Sargent/The Gazette)*

OPPOSITE PAGE: Lindsay Lawrence hugged her daughter Hayley, 3, on Friday, June 20, when they saw their Fourth Street NW home in the Time Check neighborhood for the first time since evacuating on Tuesday, June 10. Their home was marked with a purple tag indicating it was unsafe to enter. It was the first home Lindsay and her husband, Jonathan Lawrence, had owned. They were able to remove clothes, photos and major appliances before evacuating. *(Liz Martin/The Gazette)*

ABOVE: Max Hoeksema had just received an autographed T-shirt from Arizona Cardinal football player and former Cedar Rapids resident Kurt Warner on Tuesday, July 8, when he received birthday wishes from his son. Hoeksema, 79, of Pella, was taking a break from volunteering with flood recovery efforts on Ellis Boulevard NW in Cedar Rapids. *(Jonathan D. Woods/The Gazette)*

RIGHT: Workers from the Cotton national disaster relief company washed flood-soiled windows at the University of Iowa's Art Building West on July 8 in Iowa City. *(Brian Ray/The Gazette)*

The Gazette photo staff during the 2008 flood: left to right: Jonathan D. Woods, Paul Jensen (director of photography); Brian Ray, Courtney Sargent, Rollin Banderob (photo editor), Jim Slosiarek, Cliff Jette, Liz Martin. *(Mark Tade/The Gazette)*

Acknowledgments

Photographers: **Cliff Jette, Liz Martin, Brian Ray, Courtney Sargent, Jim Slosiarek, Jonathan D. Woods, Rollin Banderob, Angie Holmes**

Book editor: **Lyle Muller**

Photo editor: **Paul Jensen**

Design, layout: **Tara Ellison**

Writer: **Mike Hlas**

Image production: **Fran Roushar, Terri Vosmek, Shawn Dougherty**

Contributing editors: **Rae Riebe, Margaret Wagner, Rollin Banderob, Rachel Young, Angie Slosiarek**

Graphic artist: **David Miessler-Kubanek**

Marketing and project manager: **Stacie Bedford**

Gazette Communications

Chairman of the board: **Joe Hladky**

President and chief executive officer: **Chuck Peters**

Executive vice president and chief financial officer: **Ken Slaughter**

The Gazette

Publisher: **Dave Storey**

Editor: **Stephen Buttry**

Vice president/general manager of print operations: **Peg Schmitz**

Vice president of circulation: **Scott Swenson**

Special thanks

Mary Ellen Johnson, Jody Nolte, McKenzie McDonald, Stacey Stefani, Mary Sharp

Gazette customer service department

The image on a pedestrian crossing sign appeared to walk on water along North Riverside Drive near the University of Iowa Museum of Art in Iowa City on Sunday, June 15. *(Brian Ray/The Gazette)*

By the numbers

Houses damaged
Cedar Rapids: **5,283** (parcels: 5,390)
Iowa City/Coralville: **250**

Businesses damaged
Cedar Rapids: **940** (parcels: 1,049)
Iowa City/Coralville: **200** (estimate)

University of Iowa buildings damaged: **20**

City blocks
Cedar Rapids: **1,300**

Square miles
Cedar Rapids: **10**

River crests
Cedar Rapids: **31.12 feet**, June 13, at 10:15 a.m.
Iowa City: **31.53 feet**, June 15, in the afternoon

Flood stages
Cedar Rapids: **12 feet**
Iowa City: **22 feet**

One month after crests
Cedar Rapids: **8.66 feet**
Iowa City: **20.11 feet**

Two months after crests
Cedar Rapids: **4.43 feet**
Iowa City: **12.58 feet**

Previous records
Cedar Rapids: **20.0 feet** (1851, 1929)
Iowa City: **28.52 feet** (1993)

Non-profit and faith organizations damaged
Cedar Rapids: **47 non-profit and 30 faith organizations**
Iowa City/Coralville: **5 non-profit (excluding University of Iowa) and 2 faith organizations**

Dollar damage to homes (early estimates)
Cedar Rapids: **$231 million**
Iowa City: **$62 million**
Coralville: **$2.6 million**

KEY

- = 100-year flood plain
- = 500-year flood plain
- = 2008 flood boundaries

K Ave.

J Ave.

Cottage Grove Ave.

NE

E Ave.

Oakland Rd.

19th St.

Ellis Blvd.

Linden Dr.

15th St.

17th St.

Q Ave.

Blake Blvd.

Cedar Lake

Grande Ave.

Cedar River

College Dr.

380

16th St.

O Ave.

Coe Rd

Bever Ave.

13th St.

TIME CHECK

6th St.

11th St.

M Ave.

A Ave.

5th Ave.

NW

9th St.

1st St.

Ellis Blvd.

J Ave.

3rd St.

19th St.

F Ave.

1st Ave.

10th St.

Mount Vernon Rd.

E Ave.

3rd Ave.

7th St.

8th St.

B Ave.

5th Ave.

5th St.

SE

2nd Ave.

MAY'S ISLAND

3rd St.

18th St.

1st Ave.

1st St.

10th Ave.

12th Ave.

8th Ave.

3rd St.

1st St.

8th Ave.

10th Ave.

12th Ave.

NEW BOHEMIA/ OAK HILL

Otis Rd.

McCarthy Rd.

Rockford Rd.

9th St.

6th St.

4th St.

C St.

CZECH VILLAGE

Memorial Dr.

16th Ave.

15th Ave.

CEDAR RAPIDS

N

12th St.

19th Ave.

Bowling St.

SW

J St.

Wilson Ave.

CEDAR VALLEY/ ROMPOT

380

Wilson Ave.

C St.

Source: City of Cedar Rapids

Gazette map

Cedar Rapids' waste-water treatment plant on Bertram Road SE near Highway 13, not shown on this map, was overwhelmed by floodwater and out of service June 12 until June 15, when it started going back in service in phases.

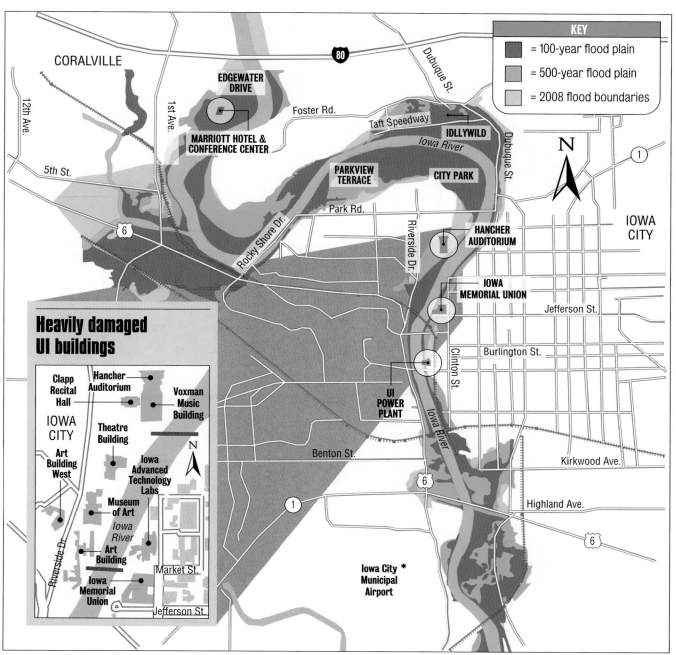

KEY

= 100-year flood plain

= 500-year flood plain

= 2008 flood boundaries

CORALVILLE

80

12th Ave.

1st Ave.

5th St.

6

EDGEWATER DRIVE

Foster Rd.

MARRIOTT HOTEL & CONFERENCE CENTER

Dubuque St.

Taft Speedway

IDLLYWILD

Iowa River

PARKVIEW TERRACE

CITY PARK

Dubuque St.

Park Rd.

Rocky Shore Dr.

Riverside Dr.

HANCHER AUDITORIUM

N

1

IOWA CITY

IOWA MEMORIAL UNION

Jefferson St.

Clinton St.

Burlington St.

UI POWER PLANT

Iowa River

Benton St.

Kirkwood Ave.

6

6

1

Highland Ave.

6

Iowa City * Municipal Airport

Heavily damaged UI buildings

Clapp Recital Hall

Hancher Auditorium

Voxman Music Building

IOWA CITY

Theatre Building

Art Building West

Iowa Advanced Technology Labs

Museum of Art

Iowa River

Art Building

N

Iowa Memorial Union

Market St.

Riverside Dr.

Jefferson St.

* Portions of the Iowa City Municipal Airport and Ralston Creek are in the 100-year flood plain but did not flood in summer 2008.

Source: Gazette research, cities of Iowa City, Coralville

Gazette graphic

Flood 2008 Timeline

Cedar Rapids

June 9
· Cedar River predicted crest: 20 feet in Cedar Rapids

June 10
· City braces for flood by sandbagging, building dirt levees

June 11
· Cedar River predicted crest: 24.7 feet
· River crest forecast gauge fails
· Northwest/southwest Cedar Rapids evacuated
· Downtown bridges close in evening

June 12
· Heavy rains produce flash floods
· Predicted crest: 32 feet
· 8,000 evacuated, including Quaker, jail, downtown Cedar Rapids
· May's Island, downtown, neighborhoods inundated
· Volunteers sandbag — and help save — city's last water well
· Thousands, including downtown, without power
· Two Red Cross emergency shelters open
· National Guard arrives

June 13
· Cedar River crests: 31.1 feet at 10:15 a.m., almost 20 feet above flood stage
· 10,000 evacuated, including Mercy Medical Center
· Water use limited to drinking
· Interstate 380 closes at Iowa River bridge
· U.S. Coast Guard arrives

June **4th** **5th** **6th** **7th** **8th** **9th** **10th** **11th** **12th** **13th**

Iowa City / Coralville

June 4
· Coralville Lake officials warn that water could overtake spillway, boost outflow
· UI evacuates Mayflower Residence Hall
· Sandbagging under way in Iowa City, Coralville

June 5
· Iowa City, Coralville neighborhoods take floodwater
· Dubuque Street closed

June 6
· Local officials say 1993 flood levels expected

June 8
· Iowa River surpasses flood stage of 22 feet

June 9
· Local officials say 500-year flood expected

June 10
· Coralville Lake goes over spillway, floodgates opened wide
· Iowa River predicted crest: 30.5 feet in Iowa City
· Coralville Lake predicted crest: 715.7 feet above sea level

June 11
· Iowa River predicted crest: 30.9 feet in Iowa City

June 12
· Iowa City's Parkview Terrace neighborhood evacuated in middle of night
· Evacuations later in day at Idyllwild neighborhood, Gilbert Street business area
· Coralville's Edgewater Drive neighborhood evacuated
· Breach in CRANDIC railbed sends Iowa River onto Coralville strip

June 13
· Coralville's Fourth Avenue neighborhood evacuated
· UI abandons nonessential operations, including classes; evacuates flood-prone buildings
· Iowa River passes 28.52-foot record, predicted crest: 33 feet
· Johnson County Administration Building closed

June 14
· Linn and Johnson counties declared federal disaster areas

June 15
· Strike teams begin entering flooded neighborhoods to determine safety
· Tempers flare when residents denied entry to their neighborhoods
· River falls to 24.3 feet — still higher than any previous flood

June 18
· Four downtown bridges reopen
· City Council sets up contractor certification system, hears pleas for buyouts

June 16
· City Hall moves to AEGON; city and county offices go to Westdale; courts move to Kirkwood

June 17
· I-380 reopens to Iowa City

June 20
· Water restrictions lifted except for industry

June 21
· River drops below 12-foot flood stage for first time since June 2

June 25
· 2,000 homes likely to be razed, city says

June 30
· Power restoration begins in downtown

July 2
· First FEMA mobile homes arrive in Cedar Rapids for temporary housing

July 7
· City cautions homeowners not to count on FEMA buyouts

July 9
· Red Cross closes one emergency shelter; local agencies take over other one

14th 15th 16th 17th 18th 19th 20th 21st 24th 25th 30th **July** 1st 2nd 7th 9th

June 14
· Coralville Lake level passes record of 716.71 feet above sea level
· Huge volunteer sandbag effort at UI, Iowa City, Coralville
· Nighttime curfew imposed for floodwater area

June 15
· Iowa River crests earlier than expected at 31.5 feet
· Coralville Lake crests at 716.97 feet above sea level
· UI officials reveal that Hancher Auditorium, among other buildings, took big hit

June 19
· President Bush visits flooded areas in Iowa City during Midwest swing

June 24
· Water stops going over Coralville Lake spillway

June 30
· Iowa City Council agrees to explore buyouts

July 1
· Coralville City Council expresses interest in buyouts

July 7
· Iowa River falls below flood stage

Index